Laurie Ann Guerrero
I Have Eaten the Rattlesnake
New and Selected Poems

Other Books by Laurie Ann Guerrero

A Crown for Gumecindo
A Tongue in the Mouth of the Dying
Babies under the Skin

Laurie Ann Guerrero
I Have Eaten the Rattlesnake
New and Selected Poems

TCU Press
Fort Worth, Texas

TCU Texas Poet Laureate Series

Library of Congress Cataloging-in-Publication Data

Names: Guerrero, Laurie Ann, author. | Espada, Martín, 1957- writer of
  introduction.
Title: I have eaten the rattlesnake : new and selected poems / Laurie Ann
  Guerrero.
Other titles: TCU Texas poets laureate series.
Description: Fort Worth, TX : TCU Press, [2020] | Series: TCU Texas poet
  laureate series | Summary: "This is a collection of poems by a Texas
  poet laureate"-- Provided by publisher.
Identifiers: LCCN 2020038668 (print) | LCCN 2020038669 (ebook) | ISBN
  9780875657462 (hardcover) | ISBN 9780875657691 (ebook)
Subjects: LCSH: Mexican Americans--Texas--Poetry. | LCGFT: Autobiographical
  poetry.
Classification: LCC PS3607.U463 I3 2020 (print) | LCC PS3607.U463 (ebook)
  | DDC 811/.6--dc23
LC record available at https://lccn.loc.gov/2020038668
LC ebook record available at https://lccn.loc.gov/2020038669

TCU Press
TCU Box 298300
Fort Worth, TX 76129
817.257.7822

www.prs.tcu.edu
To order books: 1.800.826.8911

Designed by fusion29
www.fusion29.com

BEFORE ANYTHING, MY WARRIORS:
DREW, VIC, AND LIV.

16

contents

From *A Crown for Gumecindo*

Occasional and Ekphrastic Poems

INTRODUCTION

Laurie Ann Guerrero's poems weave a narrative of suffering and resistance to suffering in her family and in the Tejano and Mexican-American community of San Antonio. She pares the skin from the backbone of that suffering with a knife made of words.

Take the visceral title: *I Have Eaten the Rattlesnake*. This title harkens back to the first poem in the book, "On Eating Rattlesnake," and the last line of the book as well—those circles, those echoes of resilience, surviving in spite of repeated losses and traumas, flourishing as a Tejana, a woman, a mother, a poet who embraces and yet transcends these multiple identities, refusing to be boxed in. "I had to eat it. I had to know this," the poet says, as the true poets say.

How history trails behind her everywhere, made manifest in the ghosts of grandparents picking cotton in 1943, their "cotton sacks twelve / feet long / dragging behind / like a tongue."

And yet that tongue does not speak. Her grandfather remembered the terror of lynching, how that violence carved the border around his people like a mapmaker or a river, "bodies swaying above the cotton like sheets on a line." Small wonder, then, that he was "silent, like every man after him: / opening his mouth only to eat." Listen to that silence—and listen the poet did, not only to tell her grandfather's story, but also to grieve for him in an extraordinary crown of sonnets.

The mountain chain running through the heart of this book is the crown of sonnets for the poet's grandfather called *A Crown for Gumecindo*. These are mournful, lyrical, surreal poems that linger in the mind's eye long after the book closes. There is the indelible poem, "Casketing," where her grandfather's coffin follows her in every dream, sometimes to the grocery, "twice to the Fiesta Bakery / on Pleasanton," backstage at the high school play. Thus, Guerrero's nightmares become our own, which is what poets should do for us, or to us. The poems perform a critical function of the elegy: to rescue the dead from oblivion. Yet these elegies go beyond mere speaking for the dead; they, she insists, "speak for us."

Guerrero trails this history behind her like a twelve-foot sack jammed with cotton. She pushes history in front of her like her grandfather's coffin at the grocery. From all the racism, the grief, the trauma come not only healing, but tenderness. The tenderness she bestows is a necessary talisman to ward off the brutality all around them. Guerrero knows the expression of that brutality firsthand. In "Brownies of the Southwest: Troop 704," she remembers hearing as a child "the word / *beaner* /from the / white boys / who'd spit first in my broccoli, / then in my hair," the slashes throughout the poem like scarring on the page. Now, a new generation of white boys, emboldened, incited, inflamed, act out their inheritance. This is how we come to the El Paso Massacre on August 3, 2019, when one such white boy with an assault rifle murdered twenty-two human beings in his mission to stop what his manifesto called "the Hispanic invasion of Texas."

Since tenderness is necessary but not sufficient in this world, Laurie Ann Guerrero has written her own manifestos, declarations of principle and poetics, telling us what it means to be an artist in a community under attack. "Ars Política: How to Make Art" is a blood-stirring poem where the poet calls upon a history of resistance: "Be ready to cough up songs, corridos plucked first / by a revolutionary whose gun smoke you wear in your hair." She invokes ancestors, collective memories, hands that do what needs to be done:

> battle lines and color lines, birthing in the huts, in the casitas
> under a grove of mesquite and huizache,
>
> and, too, lynchings and genocide in the feathery strands
> of our DNA that move our hands to do the work.
>
> Trust your hands know the work
> even if you do not know the work.

There is a second manifesto dedicated to the three hundredth anniversary of her beloved San Antonio, "a city defeated." Here the poet invokes the power of her own warrior name, again calling on the ancestors in swirling, vivid language:

> Guerrero: let me praise
> this rain that carries in it the ashes of my grandfather,
> that in its swell through these streets feeds the mesquite.

And she celebrates struggle, especially the losses that, drop by bloody drop, year by bloody year, create change:

Teach me to praise the battles
we have lost in the clinics, in the schools, in the fields,
in the voting booth, and at the dinner table.

"Teach me," says the teacher. Indeed, the best teachers and the strongest poets know that we never stop learning from that struggle, so we can go on singing, shouting, whispering, and fighting. So it is with Laurie Ann Guerrero. Listen to this poet.

Martín Espada
March 2020

on eating rattlesnake

I remember it only once—I was small. Maybe it was
the one my father shot off the front porch, maybe it
wasn't. The men stood around the fire; the women sat
inside. I snaked around the men hiding myself:
slitherer. I have seen it many times, the long
stripping—one fist pulling skin, another pulling flesh.
And how the kills were celebrated: rattles and skins
hung like tapestries. The innards left to wild things.
When it was passed around, hot from the fire outside,
the women did not partake. I dug in, rough and
curious: there was nothing more unashamed than a
rattler. No apology in its tongue. It would never be
cute. I had to eat it. I had to know this.

from
A Tongue in the Mouth of the Dying

PREPARING THE TONGUE

In my hands, it's cold and knowing as bone.
Shrouded in plastic, I unwind its gauze,
mummy-like, rub my wrist blue against the cactus
of its buds. Were it still cradled inside
the clammy cow mouth, I should want to enchant it:
let it taste the oil in my skin, lick
the lash of my eye. What I do instead
is lacerate the frozen muscle, tear
the brick-thick cud conductor in half to fit
a ceramic red pot. Its cry reaches me
from some heap of butchered heads as I hack
away like an axe murderer. I choke down
the stink of its heated moo, make carnage
of my own mouth, add garlic.

SUNDAYS AFTER BREAKFAST:
A LESSON IN COTTON PICKING
South Texas, 1943

It was a kind
of dance: feet
shuffling in dust,

fluttering
hands like birds:
nest-building:

blood staining
brown birds red.
Cotton sacks, twelve

feet long,
dragging behind
like a tongue—

fat and slow
as sun.
I watch him:

slow weep
of his eye
remembering

the girl who'd name
and nurse
nine children.

He picks
my grandma
by the color

of her dress,
her eyes,
and because she's lucky,

not
by how much cotton
she can pick.

SUNDAYS AFTER BREAKFAST:
A LESSON IN SPEECH

There were no names for men like that—gringos
who stitched up their rules, their white garb, laced snug
the issues of the day: *Lord didn't make us to mix*

with them folk, they said. But God's got nothing
to do with black boys dumped still alive into a restless river.
God's got nothing to do with having to tell their mamas.

That bloody water ran through each dark vein across Texas,
fed the Gulf, all its brown-skinned people. This, grandpa could name:
los cuerpos—bodies swaying above the cotton like sheets on a line.

No importaba que no eras negro, pero que no eras gringo.
No, it didn't matter that you weren't black, grandpa says,
pushing himself from the table, but that you weren't white.

He lived his life this way: silent, like every man after him:
opening his mouth only to eat, holding his head above
the cotton, between white men and black boys.

Las Lenguas

Once, a man told me
to hear the voice of God
one must first be able
to speak in tongues.

Years later, another man
told me speaking in tongues
was the kind of sin
you couldn't hide.

Who knows what the priests
told my mother when, with a quivering
chin, she pleaded, *Por favor, padre,*
necesito ir al baño, squeezing
her tiny six-year-old thighs
together in the best English
she could muster.

summer

In the birdhouse grandpa made for me when I was four,
life-sized, my name convex around the ovular door, I began.
A bird of squabble, my cawing unrecognizable

in a family of boars, I'd pick the burrs off the suffocating cactus
to decorate the red Velcro shoes my mother bought at Winn's,
queening my birdhouse where no one was allowed to enter.

Not even real birds. When my father hoisted my house
a good 3 or 4 feet up on rusted barrels made for gasoline,
I used my tricycle as a staircase—even decorated the handle

bars as if it were Christmastime with wilted morning glories
and yerba buena. I fell out once, nearly to my death,
trying to keep a runaway bull from noticing the blood

red of my shoes. I could not fly. It was in the dark gray summer,
when drops of rain began to fall that I learned politics of men
and birds: we framed pictures of a black bull that played

in a pile of gravel that sat where my birdhouse used to.
I watched my house's red trim slant along the white plywood
walls smolder with the embers of a cleared brush in the early July

rain. How in the rain I loved it most. It was in the dark
gray summer, when drops of rain began to fall that I knew
the human language. My body was not my own.

stray cat

She was fat. Round as the moon,
just as gray. She didn't have time
for hiding, for safety, for hissing away
onlookers. Her legs jerked and out rolled
the little slick and wormy bundles. Two.
She circled them, inspected the mousy
ears, licked the furless pink skin.
They made no noise. Their tiny hearts rippled,
though softly. She ate one.
Then, she ate the other.

Babies under the House

In Memoriam: Siblings, Sariyah Garcia, fourteen months old
& Sebastian Lopez, four months old
San Antonio, Texas, March 2007

When you open your eyes again, Sariyah,
this'll just be one of those things—like rice and bean
tacos every night, having to go

to the free clinic, buying gas with food stamps
at Ben's Ice House at the corner of Pleasanton
and Petaluma. But you know that, don't you—

know that your body will never grow completely?
When you open your eyes, your skin will be smooth
as the day you were born, not what it was

when they found you and the tiny thing
that was your brother. The dirt around you
will have licked away mother's milk

from your lips, absorbed the sour scent of mother's
breath on your neck. The iron-heavy taste of blood
in your mouth, you won't even remember.

When you open your eyes again, Sariyah,
you will be the mother. Your tart Mexican heart
won't let you be anything else.

No need for grown-ups—Child Protective Services
who were too busy, the legislators who couldn't give
medication, education to this poor neighborhood,

this city, La Raza with no muscle, no voice. Hope
decomposing in a couple of plastic bags. But there are two
things you will have that your mother never did:

a whole Sariyah, a whole Sebastian.

MY MOTHER WOKE A ROOSTER

She wasn't surprised that morning by the stove
when she cracked open a fresh brick of coffee
with hands feathered as the bed from which she rose.
She stood there. Upon her head, the morning sun
soothed her like guitars strumming—a halo: saint:
fit for lit candle on the mantle, the dressing table.

When she walked to the sink for water,
a bouquet of blue and black and rose
rose from the coccyx, up and over like a waterfall,
swiping the sugar and cream from the counter.
She was amazed by her wide presence in the tiny kitchen,
the incredible strength in her thighs, the ease of the strut.

In a pan hanging above the stove, she caught
the reflection of herself and swooped her rubbery
coxcomb back, letting it fall over her brow.
She pursed her red lips—her mouth just visible
deep inside a sharp beak.

She watched in wonder the staccatoed swivel
of her neck, rubbing what the night before
was the wrinkled throat of an old woman.
Her eyes now fitting on the face of a fighting cock.
Her red-tipped toes now claws and rough as a rope.

put attention

Put attention, grandma would say, as if attention
        were a packet of salt to be sprinkled, or a mound
                we could scoop out of a carton like ice cream.

Put attention, put attention. Put it where? In her hands?
        In the percolator? On top of the television set
                that seeps fat red lips and Mexican moustaches?

Next to the jade Buddha? Between La Virgen and Cousin
        Pablo's sixth-grade class photo—marshmallowy teeth
                jumping out of his mouth? We never corrected her.

Like the breast, Spanish lulled grandma's tongue, as we threw
        down shards of English, laughing, for her to leap in and around.
                Put attention, put attention. Put it where?

Shall I put attention in my glass and drink it soft like Montepulciano
        d'Abruzzo? Like Shiner Bock? Horchata? Put attention.
                Ponga atención, she tried to say in our language.

Put attention somewhere large. Back into her eyes.
        In the part of her brain that doesn't remember her own
                daughters, how to make rice, translate instructions.

ODE TO MY BOOTS

Like San Antonio, bronze in the face, white
sky, timid green inlay of nopal, red flores.
I trace running stitch in swirl at the shaft,
finger the leathered sole. Like a shot of tequila,
you courage me up from the toes, delicate
grubs in tomato plants. You render me incognito
among men, ferocious among women who sit
cross-legged in their spiked disarmament.
With you, I navigate bridges; mi coyote on the border,
my twin lanterns. You wake in me the dormant cells,
the not-so-ancient history of Texas,
its women—slipping into something more:
vaquera, embroidered crown, umbilicus.
Both male and female—that knowing.

Morning Praise of Nightmares

When a steak knife fiddled against the sinew of my gut, I heard
the slow whine, felt each ridge, felt the simmering red erupt
like the juice of an overripe plum—the tickle of nectar running
down the body, still warm from the sun. And from the kitchen

to the street fair—as it often is in dreams—children laughing,
a clown, the color yellow, balloons melting against the burned
sugar of the skin. And guns—tiny, like from gumball machines—
in tiny hands. Bullets, red and green and gunmetal blue, piercing

the skin like botflies, their metal heads in deep until the offspring,
that winged blood, gently and timidly took flight. Then the peeling
of my skin: who was that crafter whose face I never saw?
That paper-maker, his teacup hands, his clothespin fingers

rinsing clean the lace of my forearms, the squared-off torso,
long sheet of leg, thick bit of finger and toe like strips of bacon,
strung up, decorating that red room like black and white photos
developing mountains or smiles or sex. I could taste my own blood,

though I couldn't lift my hands to finish the job—put myself
out of misery. I was but remains—a piled heap of slop
on the floor of a house I never shared a meal in. Even my eyelids
were gone and my spine exposed. I was an afterbirth without

the birthing, a too-early puppy whose whole pink body thumped
with each beat of his slow heart. This is my morning praise
of nightmares: *Open your eyes*, I hear three mouths whisper
against the flower of my skull, *mama, open your eyes*.

WOODEN BOX

He demands this. Nothing
else. No mahogany slick,
or roses kissed by lilies. No
music or speech. Weeping,
limited. We are to file down
the aisle, nod head to his dead body,
return home to care for things
still living. We are not
to sob for the child
him, the bed- and alphabet-less
picker of cotton,
potatoes, tomatoes.
Follower of crops.
We are not to sob for the cactusman-
vaquero-lover him. Grandpa
who takes his milk from the moon,
who knows the time
for cookie,
the time for wine,
no.
When he is gone,
he will be gone.
I can make the box
myself, he says.
I can make it myself.

MR. G'S COLLECTION

In the CT scan, the tripas look like snakes
and one kidney dwarfs its once identical twin.

I see the lump, a wing bud, between his spine
and shoulder: this is not the cancer, says the doctor:

But tissue. A growth: Manteca: Fat.
Pregnant back full of children.

Collection of wounds, skinned over like a pie.
The many-cheated deaths: water for drowning,

horse hooves, guns, flipped up pick-ups,
booze to fill a young man's veins: flask. Cask.

All of it held up there: burden. World on his shoulder.
A monkey. Nest of wrongs, of worms. A blister.

Meatloaf. Coffee hardened to a brick.
Soap. Cake. A womb in which to grow

watermelon. A pot of beans. A dozen tamales.
He'll tell you it's a bag of money.

There, says the doctor, pointing
to what looks like the apple core we threw

off the jetties in the Corpus Christi Bay
when I was four, bobbing in grandpa's stomach

with each breath he takes: *there's the cancer.*

ODE TO EL CABRITO

More than sheep and cow
and butterfly, I love you.
No envy between us
like the rooster-footed.
In your belly, I live
like warm milk, goat-
thick and cloud heavy,
lick you from the inside
until the slaughter—when your mother
cries like my mother. When fire
sends its last breath to the stars,
I tear away your muscle, bubbling
fat, and warm tortillas over coal.
In the onion and cilantro,
you do not recoil like the burnt skin
of the pig, but spread yourself: sunbather.
The rest of you still on the spit,
gap-mouthed, your fleshless
head tossed back:
you love being loved.
In the sweet meat of you—
little hooved, little horned—
I taste my own skin.

Ancient Algebra

after Erin Margaret Oliver

I.

Danger − "brain" = me ∴ ♀ + "brain" = dangerous

       x (bonemeal + modulation) = silence

x = {Fire, ♀}

If x = {Fire, ♀}, then x (danger)$^{(DEGRADATION)}$ = quest for "brain"

             Conquest + cotton + cactus − "brain" ≤ ♀

             God + milk + eyes - silence ≥ ♂

                   {(Quest for brain) *(∞) = deprivation}

II.

♀ + ♂ = modification of the womb; bonemeal reconstituted

                 {∞ = √ womb}

What you call my children ≠ what I call my children

        <u>modulation (quest for "brain" + colonization of the poetic)</u>

               My children

       y = revolution

revolution ≠ "education" + quest for equality

quest for equality >> ("education")(∞)

                             Solution = Ø

Early Words For My Son

You will probably make sense of it all some Wednesday
        afternoon as you sit with your wife and daughters,
                unbuckling leather footlockers, poems,

your mother's curvy schedule, knowing then
        why I never taught you anything but how to read
                and how to shade by crosshatching at the lip,

under the cheekbone, on the portraits
        you made of me. You will probably thank me,
                post-puberty, for never sitting down,

sparing you "the talk." You will learn the way I claimed to—
        some girl named Suzie who will also teach you to smoke.
                It took a long time before your father understood,

and who knows what the hell I'll tell your sisters.
        But you should know that when we were lonely,
                and you nine, wanting me to hold you,

I just couldn't do it with my arms. You were born male
        like I was born female, and all I've ever known
                is how to carry you in my teeth.

one man's name: colonization of the poetic

> Bridges are thresholds to other realities, archetypal,
> primal symbols of shifting consciousness. . . . [They] span
> liminal spaces between worlds, spaces I call nepantla,
> a Náhuatl word meaning tierra entre medio [land in between].
> —Gloria Anzaldúa

i.

This is the womb
From which my children came
This is the skin I use to feel. These feet
     above us.

There are the men
Those white beards
    Wave like flags in the sky

Walk the land. With these hands, I straighten
The spines of my children.
On this bridge

    They were given to live.

      There are the men who line up ships.

ii.

The night we stood in a circle around you, a god,
poetry rising like fire to meet our mouths,
you asked about the babies I've birthed.
Wine-heavy, wise, gold-seeking
god, you redheaded Cortéz in a circle:
you ask about my babies, ask if they carry

    one man's name.

The white hair on your chest fingers me closer,
your gold blood, gold chain, feathered serpent
in the skin of an old man: I waited for you: Wine-

    heavy me, Malinchista.

iii.

Did you see me in San Antonio
at seventeen, my legs like the battle-worn door
of Mission San Jose: open: one baby St. Jude's,
one baby St. Andrew's, one baby fathered by the father
of St. Anne. Since my birth, they tell me
you are my father, your white mouth
teaching me how to speak: Cortéz.

Hail Mary.

    Blessed art thou amongst women.

iv.

Let them rip the heart
from the fighting cock, stitch
their skins together tight to protect
the unexplored bridge.
Let them know the land, blood
that runs deep to its center.
Let them lead their brother.

Fight is the birthright of my daughters, two.

v.

The night we stood in a circle
wine-heavy, you, our gold god,
fair-haired and bearded, you sacrificed
my children like the Aztecs

      they are.

Line up the bearded men. Get in line.

vi.

When you shove yourself into my throat,
the words I know become foreign, jagged.
A new race forms between the soft palate
and the base of my tongue. A pregnant mouth,
I carry you there, where words form:

    I sew flags like babies.

vii.

My grandmother embroidered huipiles.
Named me the color of stone, lavender
in the sun. Wore a herd of elephants
on her middle finger, the baby always
almost dead. In white cotton thread on pink
cotton dress, she stitched swans to their heads,
made bloom red roses and the white-flowered
Mala Mujer. She birthed nine children.
She sits now in a room where the faces are familiar
as snow and the hands that feed her are not her own.

She wears your name, a crown, Cortéz:
queen of a tongue no one understands.
What have you done?

viii.

Cortéz is my mother's name, too. Conquista,
the iron and arms she gave me to lock
myself up tight were stolen by the boy
who sells candy apples, bottled water
at the corner of Military & Flores.
He wears my armor under a new sun
and sweats in Náhuatl.

Grandma sees him in her dreams.

ix.

Write the body well, I say.
Pink man, write well, write body.
Little pink man: write books,
write history, white history: Cortéz
and I have the same hands: grandmother.
Bodies ripped with babies and men: molcajete:
pounded, blood-red dust, pigment
for painting. Art. Framed in gold.

from
A Crown for Gumecindo

where the dead come to speak

El Paso, Texas/Ciudad Juárez

in this way
     could she

—Valerie Martínez
from *Each and Her*

And maybe there was a Laurie Ann who left
behind three children, a sink full of dishes,
a man who kissed her as if the whole world
lived in her mouth. And maybe, too, her heart
was carved out from underneath the cradle

of her rib. The ocotillo motions
with its strange arms: death goes on. I conjure
you in bootsoles and sand, ice and humming
—bird, borderwalker and little girl.

Have you found my likeness on the other side,
        I memorized your hands when I was six years old.
as I search for you here? I thought you'd be
alone. You are not alone. Hadn't they
their own fathers to heed—saying, as mine
has said, don't be alone, don't cross the line?

LOVE IS OUR MOTHER

You said, *don't be alone. Don't cross the line*,
girl—the potential in my hands to raise Hell,
you knew before I did. We were never good

but to each other: the brain creates
its devil: in this dream, he makes me choose
which of us will die by the hand of the other
and which of us will carry the dead home:
You kill the boy or the boy kills you, he says.

In this dream, my steady hands are not my own:
your hands load the gun: you know I cannot
let him live: his bones cannot hold the weight
of me. With my eyes, I see your hands. My eyes
see the boy I birthed—my jaw that quivers.
You wake me before you pull the trigger

PRAISE SONG FOR THE GOAT AT THE GRAVE

You woke me before you pulled the trigger—
tempting songs from your guitar—late night, after
cabrito plucked from its mother's body,
in praise of September rain: we ate. Praise
September, praise rain—though I can still taste
merciless July. At your grave, I nestle

hard candies in wet earth as to return
diamonds, as to sow seeds. I want your tongue
to wind its way through the hinged lip of casket,
black rock, pull them down to your softened teeth.

Who knows what you're capable of now—what grows
now that your heart has fed the dirt. But only
goats are here—bleating songs I do not know.
Only the goats are here to say hello.

THE ABSENCE OF WATER

Only the goats are here to say hello
when I kneel at your grave. I straighten blue
ribbon from your casket, wipe dust settled
in plastic red roses: your headstone has
not arrived. I rearrange rocks, pull newborn

weeds that sprout like vocal chords: he's dead,
they hum. In my nails, your dirt burrows like worms.
> I watched my tear fall into the lining of your blue casket.
> I watched my tear fall near your shoulder and disappear
> into the fabric, fast, like a raindrop into the thirsty earth.

My hands are dirty and you are not here

in your blue jeans, with your slow eye, to throw
me a manguera, to rinse my hands, to
wet my lips, to bless the little bodies
of tomatoes—trying to follow a sun
they can't see, shrinking, puckered on the vine,
shaking in their skins, faces split as mine.
> Take me with you.

THE mesquite

Aching in their skins, faces split as mine,
the mesquite knows best: you died entirely
without me. There is a new kind of crying:
an untold red I have never known. Tears,

like mercury in the hollow of my
belly, like water burning through a well.
I hear the slosh as if I am a child
swollen with milk. In bed, I cradle my
own belly—ripe with an unnamed infant.

The mesquite separates us with his thin
finger. Before our births, he was coming
for us. I do not love mesquite—his old
skin, his cold, brown face, tangled, and worn through—
like yours, mi muerto, the last time I saw you.

WITHOUT YOU, I am cactus

Like yours, mi muerto, the last time I saw you,
October's eyes are gray. Today, you are
not a dead man: October resurrects.
Today your blood, my blood, fills the private
rooms of my barbed and thorny limbs. I have
come to love October in the name of you.

Today, I say, you're back. Today, swallow rain.
Today, I soften on the earth; you emerge
from it. Today, I breathe life into your
dead lung. Today, I am God. Today, I
beat marrow into your bones. Today, yours
are the hands that pull spines from my spine.
Today, I shed my cactus skin for flood;
we'll look at our reflection in the mud.

newborns

Let's look at our reflection in the mud:
see how, in four months, each of us has changed.
What is your name without a body? My name
without you here? I am new: what I never
was. Suddenly, I carry my newborn

grief like a new mother—I nurse and swaddle
my most fragile, my newest, my sweet. What
festers in the bellies of strangers does not
concern me. There is only this: I am
the only mother. Mine is the only child.

I decompose alongside you, wanting
and not wanting everyone to see me—
off-balanced and leaking, my skin in strands—
the oddity that was put in my hands.

DÍA DE LOS MUERTOS

El Carmen Cemetery, Bexar County, Texas

The oddity that was put in my hands—
your truck. It used to be I drove this road
each week to pick you up. Now I drive this road
each week to lay you down again. Today
is the day of the dead: When did you die?

Today I bring you chicharrón con huevo,
chile. Which is to say, I brought breakfast
to the goats. I want to slip my hand into
the photo of you, fix your hair as I did,

help you with your sweater, guide heavy salt
to your plate. Grass is starting to grow over
you. Shards of rock gone smooth. I sing to bees.
I lay my ear to stone; it doesn't hurt:
I hear your song—water rising from dirt.

SUNDAY DINNER

I hear your song—water rising from the dirt
of Sunday. I peel potatoes for your
> The coming out is abrupt:
> I am singing to the red bird (you are

dead) mouth. I wear your teeth like an apron,
bandolier across my chest. I only
know how to feed you and fire. I think

> I am making a meal for the children (you are dead).

I've lost my children, too. I look for you
in salt, in the red meat of sun. My children
are soldiers, lined rows of corn, ears wrapped in silks,
> I have decided to comb my hair (you are dead).

faces tucked in stalks. They have learned the war
of keeping: we trudge through the mud of Sunday.
At the table, we take from each other's
> What was the name of . . . (you are dead).
> I can bring you pan dulce (you are dead).

faces—little fires. When you were here,
I didn't know to serve the meal this way.
> (You are dead.)

stone Fruit

Good? I would ask. *Good enough*, you would say
of the wine we made from plums. Didn't we,
for years, tend the mothertree? Didn't we,
for years, prune, pluck, hold in our hands the purpled
bodies bursting, that begged: *me next, have me?*

Weren't we so nourished in the nerve? Someone
is buying our tree. You are reduced to pit.
I put seed in dirt, wait for you to come
back to me in a jar by the window.
You are not growing. Aren't you a plum?

Little red, little kidney, little mouth
singing, calling: *I'm here! I'm here!* I thought
the dirt would give you something to take hold of:
I've buried everything I've ever loved.

CASKETING

I've buried everything I've ever loved
in the bone of reason: now, even in dreams
you are dead. Sometimes, I wheel your metal–
colored coffin to the grocery store.

Once, to a paperie. Twice to Fiesta
Bakery on Pleasanton. You are heavy.
Once, I was in high school, in a play, and parked
you stage left. Always, I shake you: Wake up,
damn you. Sometimes, the casket is open

and I kick you. And when, in my small shoes,
I make contact, your ribs crumble like the bark
of an old mesquite: *wake up, wake up!* We can't
run the numbers, argue, make your mother's bread
if you are always going to be dead.

UNTOUCHABLE

If you are always going to be dead,
who then will melt away the breasts from my
chest? Need more my eyes than the unraveling
of my hips? In your house, I was all bedrock
and teeth. Cutthroat. Stopped clock—just as much man
as woman. Or rain. You were blind and I loved
you for it. In your house, my shoulders grew

to fit the work. Patience blossomed upon
my head: a crown. You were my mirror: my name,
ready plum of my right hand, my ancient
and river'd neck, my compass, my wing, my
open gate, my warrior, my sleepless legion—

as if I had been born male: my kingdom come.
And one day in hot July, my kingdom gone.

I dream a room with small cows. Your youngest grandson and I wipe
the snow from their tiny hides. They fit in the palms of our hands. We
rub clean their hooves, their tails like thread. When I pile them into
a nest, little black and white bovine, they are rats. I try to hide my
shock, my disgust. I need to find the answer. What is the question?

Finally, in a country store, I see a man with a beard. A cowboy. His
long legs lead me to a hall. I know him. He is my uncle, dead one year.
In a room, he is sitting on a bed: *Mija*, he says, *what is your question?*

Uncle, I say, *I am so sad.*

THE WORK: BLUEPRINTS FOR THE BODY

One day in hot July, my king, you were gone—
wheeled out under the red and early sky.
Until you find me, I build a house: carve
boulders with your chisel, sweep fire and air
aside with sage, dig tunnels with my hands.

What are you preparing for? they ask. I keep
working. If a dog in my path bares his teeth,
I eat him whole. Ten months in, I am almost
done: stones are flat. I've mastered the level,

T—square, carved my own name in the handle
of my own hammer. A spider returns
to the center of her web—how will you come?
Muscle or rain? I have, 'til you come down,
only the page from which to build this crown.

en las costillas de la página

Only the page on which to place your crown—
ink–soaked reliquary: here goes your hat,
your skin, my love, my Gumecindo. Grandpa,

meet me here all my life. Let us gather
together in the ribs of the page—I will
bare myself in the soft curve of your name.
I will loosen, unbolt hinges from my nape.
Let spill the garden you would have me tend:

praise the perfect hand of each artist, each
perfect work, each perfect loss in every field
we know or do not know; mark the unringed
finger of your left hand, speak names unspoken—
the pulling apart of one from another.

Let the record be the muse for the craft:
Where else shall we live, Laurie Ann? What's left?

GOODBYE SONNET

And yes, I am the Laurie Ann you left,
who begged: Don't go alone. Don't cross the line.
         Aren't you a plum?
I've learned to keep my finger off the trigger,
         How many times did you say
         that to me? How many times?
spare the goats who've come to say hello,
shaking in their skins, faces split like mine—
like yours, mi muerto, the last time I saw you
         sing

I look for your reflection in the mud,
         Let me say your name again:
that oddity that was put in my hands.
         Gumecindo.
I hear your song—water rising from dirt:
Good? I ask. *Good enough*, you say.

I've buried everything I've ever loved:
         Gumecindo
You are always going to be dead.
         I sing to bees:
         Gumecindo
         Gumecindo

One day in hot July: my king you were gone—
only the page on which to place your crown.

Occasional and Ekphrastic Poems

LAST MEAL: BREAKFAST TACOS, SAN ANTONIO, TEJAS

after Chuck Ramirez's "Breakfast Tacos"
from the series Seven Days, 2003

Let me be your last meal.
Let me harvest the notes
I took from your mother's
watery hands, street vendors
in Rome, Ms. Rosie
from our taquería, you:
in the sun, in the open air,
let me give you zucchini
and their elusive blossoms—
my arms, my hands.
Pumpkiny empanadas
of my feet, pulpy as a newborn's.
Guisada'd loin of my calf
muscle. On a plate white
and crisp as the ocean,
lemoned eyeballs like two
scallops. The red, ripe
strawberry of my mouth.
Perhaps with coffee,
you'd have the little lobe
of my ear sugared as a wedding
cookie. The skin of my belly,
my best chicharrón, scrambled
with the egg of my brain
for your breakfast tacos.
My lengua like lengua.
Mi pescuezo, el mejor hueso.
Let me be your last meal:
mouthfuls of my never-to-be-digested
face, my immovable femur
caught in your throat like a fishbone

Let the symphonies of your
cells, your systems, quiet down,
submit to the dirt, fuse themselves
to mine. Let my body be
what could never leave your body.

HOW TO SACRIFICE YOUR SON

after "The Three Soldiers" by Frederick Hart
bronze sculpture, 1984

1. Birth him.

2. Nurse him in the crook of your teenaged arms.
    His blood more tempered than his hands.

3. Arm him with salt from your womb. Your tendency
    toward soft, kiss the tiny fingers he'll wrap around
    triggers made for killing boys.

4. Send him into the world, a hive unto himself of passion
    and almost inextinguishable light salvaged
    from the sad brown men whose names we wear.

5. Distill what is sweet from your language
    for his. Teach him, *mama, ball, doggy, fight.*

6. Let him ask you *why.* Teach him allegiance
    to the city that raised him, the apple lodged in his throat.
    He'll learn his skin is a shade lighter than his sister's.

7. Let him move about in a world
    that has him marked _____.
    Little goat, little boy bait.

8. I am telling you: you are not the victim.
    You are accomplice to his murder.

BROWNIES OF THE SOUTHWEST: TROOP 704

after "Humanscape 62" by Melesio Casa
acrylic on canvas, 1970

Three years before I'd hear the word / beaner /
from the / white boys / who'd spit first in my broccoli,
then in my hair, / my mother / dressed me

each Wednesday in that / brown / sheath: I was seven.
It'd be the only time I'd wear a sash—
Miss / America, / she said.

Twenty Miss / Americas, we made /
kitsch from clothespins, pipe cleaners—
our / brown / socks / banded and complicated /

with orange tassels just below the / brown /
/ rosettes / of our knees, little / skulls /knocking
together in our elementary / school / cafeteria.

How we jumped the day / we heard / voices
raising there instead of / at home, / when Tracy's
mom slapped our / troop / leader / and Tracy

cried. And Tracy's / mom was white /
and only her / dad was brown / and Tracy
was a little / prettier than the rest of us. /

At the lunch tables, / *white bitch* / stuck to our fingers
like glue; / *fucking Mexicans* / landed like glitter
onto the sashes laid across our / small / hearts. /

With Tracy, / we watched / manifest between us
/ a line, / risen from the tiled floor where / we shared /
meals as tears clung to the eye-rims of my seven-year-old

/ compañeras. / Lorena chewed her nails 'til blood
/ bloomed / on her ring finger. Andrea peed quietly
/ on her brown knee / socks. None of us knew

where to hide. This was not / home, /
where / we could run / to the / broom / closet
or to the / feet / of our big / brothers. /

(TO THE) YOUNG GIRL ON A CHAIR

after "Young Girl on a Chair" by Giacomo Manzú
bronze sculpture, 1955

They will find a way to bind you. Always.
Some will say it's an art. To some, it is.
To lock you in is to lock themselves in
as they were once, too. You are the bridge
between good and bad. They like it here.

They will expose you as if it's their right.
Pour the hot fire. Sand. Score the tedious layers,
the days of wax, make escapes for the tiny
imperfections caused by man in the name
of artful budding your body does on its own.
As if it might not have been preserved
otherwise. As if only tools and experience
could name you, put fire to you: *Stop here*,
he says. *Stop here, child, before you grow.*
Before you know things.
Before you know better.

There are no veins beneath the bronze.
The spiraled hair caught in the casting is not yours.
The needy face caught in the casting is not yours.
I will not visit you in this garden.
I will not praise you in the open air.

THE MINIATURE WORLD OF FAITH

after "The Doll's House: The Miniature World of Faith Bradford," 1967
National Museum of American History

I will travel the country. I will cry. I will carry
my dead with me until I no longer see my own reflection.

In the east, I will find myself in the smallest house
in the smallest corner of a stranger's name. I will give myself
to a city I hope can love a small thing. I am a small thing.

In the west, I will sip tequila from a small coffee cup
that reminds me of my dead. I will say his name with each sip
in a small city he once loved.

In the east, I am not afraid of dying. I'm afraid of being dead
and decide: I don't want to be like him—dead.
And if I don't breathe, time will stop and he will be dying,
     but not dead,
and we will sit at a small table with a small dog and a small vase
     of roses.
I will fill in the gaps of his memory with small stars I will pull
from the rose's small and indiscernible petals.

In the west, I will fall back into the near-empty bowls that contained
the freshest kind of sadness—at seven or 18—the youngest
kind of bride who could not love her husband that first night.
What did I know that I did not know? I cried for my dolls.
I cried for my own house. In the west, I am afraid.

A woman should know how to build her own house.
A woman should know which cities weaken her.

I will wind my own tears like thread on a bobbin.

I will make an archive for the unclean gossamer carried in the battered beaks of birds.

I will memorize the map home—rise from my own grave where I have slept 7 years.

I will host, in my own house, the unnamable truths of women.

I will name them.

Ars Politica: How to make art

in praise of the working artists of San Antonio, Texas,
commissioned by the City of San Antonio Department of Arts & Culture, 2016

You must start small as our mothers were small.
Our fathers, too, small.

In a pillowcase whip-stitched with roses
or in an old coffee can, collect your abuelos'

teeth; assure them you will not bury them
near the bones of the dog that froze

the winter that dogs froze.
Carry the teeth under your tongue.

Let them root there.
This is how you will learn to speak.

Be ready to cough up songs, corridos plucked first
by a revolutionary whose gunsmoke you wear in your hair.

The songs will be new in your throat. We are always
beginning. We are always beginning again.

You cannot be afraid to unhinge the jaw—
let the sun blister your mouth. Know thirst.

Cast your own eyes from their sockets like a confettied April
that you will know the bloom and battle of flowers.

Let your ribs draw across the ribs of another: el canto del violín
Let your fingers dance: el guitarrón.

Needle or pen, brushed oil, machete or drum, leather,
cilantro, stomp—be patient in the tooling,

the weaving of experience one hundred, five hundred,
ten thousand years to here: love-making in the cotton and nopal,

battlelines and colorlines, birthing in the huts, in the casitas
under a grove of mesquite and huizache,

and, too, lynchings and genocide in the feathery strands
of our DNA that move our hands to do the work.

Trust your hands know the work
even if you do not know the work.

You do not speak for the dead.
The dead speak for you.

THree HunDreD years BeFore THese, THree HunDreD aFTer

a manifesto for the celebration of the
tricentennial anniversary
of a city defeated

I come to clean the headstones that bear my names.
There is no one else I wish to speak to when I walk

away from the stove where I cook for my children
the beans I ate when I was a child. Gonzales:

with each candle I light with my conqueror hand,
let me praise my warrior feet in my city that is your body

that is my body: when the child leaves it, let us not forget
how to love him: let not, my San Antonio, forget that it is

home. I am a home. My children are caught in their studies—
spread across the city, the country, and still, though mine

is not the only hand that will feed them, I cook their beans.
Martinez: let me wear the bootsoles of every man

who walked here, in whatever color skin he was born into,
that when I walk, my milk may let in honor of his mother.

You are his mother. I am his mother. What are we to do
in times like these but remain steady? Guerrero: let me praise

this rain that carries in it the ashes of my grandfather,
that in its swell through these streets feeds the mesquite.

That I am mesquite. I only want to feed my children.
I only want to speak to my dead. Velasquez: when you left

the classroom, the churchyard, the factory, tight in your army
greens, and felt your finger numb against the trigger,

did you tether your soul to the wild rose, to the soul of a lover
who may or may not reach your heaven? When the fire fills the sky,

call me lover. I know you understand this: though others cannot
hear us, it is not because we aren't singing.

Cortez: correct in me the honoring of gold in our city,
gold faces and gold names, and gold hair, and gold shields,

and gold texts, and reliquaries of gold holding golden rings,
and histories so gold we celebrate the longing for gold

as our birthright. I am, too, a fair-haired, gold-seeking god.
I know you hear me. Tejeda: teach me to praise the battles

we have lost in the clinics, in the schools, in the fields,
in the voting booth, and at the dinner table.

That when I walk away with my children, I am still walking.
I must keep walking. Threadbare, my San Antonio—do not erase me.

German-green eyes of my Tejano father, white skin of my Tejana
     mother,
my Spanish names, my Mexican mouth, my native and beating heart—

San Antonio is a city, whole. I am a city, whole. Let my revolution be
to sing graveside, to whisper intention into bowls of beans, to dance

without fear or fight. San Antonio is made of language: mightiest
tongue, mightiest voice—let me let go that pride.

SO SHE WOULD NOT WATCH HIM SPLIT IN TWO, A MOTHER COMMITS HER CHILD TO THE CARE OF HER ENEMY

Reliquary: blue champlevé enamel on copper and wood, depicting the Judgment of King Solomon (ca. 1200-1210), Smith College Museum of Art

Not this—no reliquary and its depictions, its barren womb, its flaking face, no. No more, no less holy than a bit of bone or cloth of the forgotten dead. No man as king or woman as weigh scale. No infant child's body to split between mothers or nations. No baby on a blue box, in a box, in a cage. No relinquishing of a mother's mothering to the curators of law. Make no reliquary of the cold night, a campaign, or of desolation. Make no reliquary of the river, the system, the otherland, or dream. Make no reliquary of amendments, sword sheaths, or armories. Children, like water, will take the shape of what holds them—we are not in things.

Between the soil and the sun

in honor of the tenth anniversary of Texas A&M University-
San Antonio for Cecilia Macias & Sabrina San Miguel

". . . you cannot afford to think of being here to receive an education:
you will do much better to think of being here to claim one.
The difference is that between acting and being acted-upon.
. . . it can literally mean the difference between life and death."

-Adrienne Rich from "Claiming an Education" 1977

This is what I want to tell you:
This is yours—the air and all who breathe it.
We belong to each other, you see.

You need not carry the stones in your heart
any further. Here, there is no paper, no
number, no fight you need to produce

so that someone else will make space
for you. It's the history in your hands
that builds, brick by brick, the rooms

into which you walk. We will mark the days
as they come: a job lost, another child gone,
lines—to vote, to eat, to pay our debts—

conferring, as it were, temperance noted
in books our people could not read. Look here,
this is what I want to say: you are not here

to receive your education, but to build upon
the lessons distilled through generations
and to give your own inherent knowing

in return—in the name of something far greater.
In the spirit of yours and mine whose bodies
hold up the soles of our feet and whose knowing

tames the quiver in our throats. Here is the lot,
cleared, and in its place, the documented
evolution of our work on this land: our breath

in contracts with the earth and with each other.
You are the bloom that holds the root, making
magic between the soil and the sun.

New Work (2015-2019)

on eaTInG raBBIT

I remember it only once—I was small. I don't know
where it came from, who skinned it, how it was
caught, but that I only ever held one in my hands:
I was four and loved it despite its inability to love
me back. I wanted and did not want to hold it—such
indifference in its eyes, its wanting to be left alone,
unable to transform itself to wolf or lion. This is the
way of the rabbit, little bunny: the misunderstood,
misrepresented by fluff and cotton tail. Its work had
nothing to do with me. Nothing to prove, the rabbit
would rather die. I had to eat it. I had to know this.

mourninG sonG

Always I wake with one less
bone in my body. I do not recognize

the sound of my own crying, ancient
in its texture, inherited shrill.

Seas evaporate from my mouth.
I've begun to resemble an old shoe

whose leather is no longer malleable.
Time comes to me in suitcases, in cans

of soda. I have lost my desire to understand
numbers. All words have been invented;

old ones have lost their meanings.
To ask someone to help me

stomach the decomposition of you
with their own nervy heart

is to ask someone to help me
examine the moon

with the insides of a cactus.
I'm starting to think

the tones in my voice—indefinable scales—
are the components of a new language

for those who have fewer bones
in their throats, missing

vertebrae and mandibles:
song for the dead.

I'm afraid
I will never stop.

where I will not let you take me

I dream myself a pomegranate. What I find is brilliant: jeweled honeycomb, little wombs buzzing, a seeded market in red. I take one at a time into the cave of my mouth, propped open by tiny, top-hatted, ringleaders. My mouth is a circus. I want/don't want to eat them—the arils—translucent as newborns. Some, I lick upon its thin skin, top of each head, return them to my womb: I am a mother. But I reach for another; crush down the little men and reach for more. I can't stop myself. I grind down—seed-swallowing, seed-spilling. Handfuls. I am a monster: this is my own body. I am a circus. A white man is looking for a little girl. I am a little girl. My hands and teeth are stained red: I am bad. I am not bad. The walls of my stomach, I cannot keep shut. I hold my thick red skin, flapping, against the rib. My body is numb. My skin is drying out. It has become too small. Between the spine and the pelvic bone, nestled seeds start to dislodge. My teeth, little rubies, fall from my mouth. My toes break and roll away: I am leaving a trail. When he finds me, he ties my small ankles to two chairs. He is drunk. His shirt is stained red from the girl before me. I can't even cry. I don't much care. I was already rotting in the yard when he snatched me.

La mano ponderosa

I carry my father's guns in my grandma's blue
suitcase, away, to the home of my tía who acts

like she has never seen a gun. I am fourteen.
I am raped under a portrait of La Virgen. My fingers

tell a story: I will never hold a gun to your head:
There is no grace in a trembling hand.

I learned the rules early: You don't pull a gun
unless you're going to use it.

My grandfather says I am just like him: fighting
my shadow. Shadowboxing, I correct him.

No, he says.

One Thousand Days After Death

I dream your small and decomposed body
in my arms. When I glance down
at your face, darkened and shriveled,
I almost don't recognize you.

Words do not occupy your mouth.
No ideas in your hands. If there was a soul
inside this brittle and stiff version of you,
there is not one now.

At times, I lay you down, break open your arms
to wrap them around me. Other times, I change
your clothes—the blue button-down for the gray—
so as to keep you presentable.

The weight of your small head is familiar
in the crook of my arm, and I love you
as I love my own grown and fighting son,
once small and noiseless in my arms.

And when your face, leathered, knocks against
my breast, I think of my lover's face, dark against
my breast—how I love him with your wisdom,
little dead thing: I do not need you

to speak to me. It is enough that you are here
still. It is enough that you choose me.
It is enough that the only man
who will not leave me is a dead one.

LETTER TO MY CHILDREN ABOUT THE MOUTH

To My Son:

> If she lets you, always
> kiss the girl. But always
> kiss her softly. The mouth
> of a girl—no matter what
> poison she has tasted, spit
> forth—is the small womb
> that breeds the whole world.
> Do not think you deserve
> her mouth more even
> than she.

To My Daughters:

> When they go to kiss you,
> if you have so allowed,
> if you have not kissed them
> first, remember it's the rope
> of your voice that holds
> your bones together. Remember
> each perfect note, each dissected
> vein, each blossom of thought
> is shared through that mouth.
> And share, share—what better
> gift? If they are aggressive, you need
> not wait. You already know
> the delicacy, the gift
> of your many, many tongues.

PLAY THE SONG

—after Gwendolyn Brooks,
from "The Children of the Poor"

When I am gone, play the song. What
hum from boxes, from your small throats shall
unhinge the grief from your jaws, feed you more than I

ever could. Play the song when I can no longer give
beat, wrap my gray skin around ballad or blues. When my
hands, like leaves, shake themselves loose, my children,

when there is no more crescendo'd mother who
loved you, play the song. Play the song when all others are
filled with milk and money. Who can say that we were poor?

Inside This Hour

I want to teach your hunger
to wander, your skull
to open to the night sky.
But I am more ocean
than I am your mother.
Inside this hour,
you will know the taste
of brown skin, the massacre
in and of borders, goodbye
and earth. You will want
to leave me. I will want
to let you.

Her English name is Krissy
Changsha, China, Hunan Province

In the museum, in Changsha, we ruminate over artifacts she herself has never seen: Lady Dai's mummified skin, rice bowls that existed through one dynasty after another, the embroidered Nüshu—secret women's writing, maps of ancient China where she finds her family's village and smiles for the first time. She is especially beautiful in this moment.

I refuse to believe her history is older than mine, but say nothing. She is young—my son's age—and not here with me to contemplate my maps, my villages, my embroidered languages. Still, though she never looks me in the eye, she tells me I am beautiful, and begs me to take her umbrella to protect my skin from darkening in the hot Chinese sun.

I know nothing.

She translates placards for me, answers, in whisper, questions about Mao, and not until I eat the fermented street tofu, take her umbrella, she offers something most personal: her foot to size up against my own.

You are lucky, she says.
Small foot, light skin.

CATALYST FOR A DAUGHTER-IN-LAW

There were parts I never
wanted to speak of. The child

widening me from the inside
made of me a stage. My breasts,

two mounds of clay, and you spoke
on his behalf and for every mother—

once and future, my own and yours.
I took the wash cloths

to my nipples, each bath,
in the weeks before he came—

toughening them up as you said
I should, that they would not be too soft,

too weak for the ravenous mouth
of a boy whose face I'd never seen.

I tried. I tried to love the natural
thing. Leading a would-be-man

to my breast. I do not blame you,
mother of the one I loved: all of us

children. And god himself—
fucking you at the pulpit.

ODE TO THE BEET

Ruby-jewel, you are hard-brained, and your mouth never tells its own tales: you are quiet—no matter how I tease: pluck your wispy beard, chop the wooly top. Red water pools on the bamboo of my board, between the heavy ridges of my knife, under the pile of brown skins peeled exactly: I listen and you listen. In the chopping, I expect blood out of each piece. I expect a soft heart like the artichoke. I want to see explode the red all over my kitchen. Gush, seedy, like the innards of a tomato. Your quiet intimidates me. And no matter the oil, how small I chop, how I scrape your flesh, you live with your red like this: flesh and blood and bone are one: unconquerable beet, holding your red in your rib: the good and all the bloodied bad. There is no diluting you. No abolishing. No erasing. We consume each other like sisters.

NIGHT FEEDING

I noticed one first in the mirror—
its violet pigmentation, curved
base ascending to its volcanic eye.

An underdeveloped fetus growing
out the head of its twin, a third breast
to the left of my left nipple at this age

like an unwanted pregnancy. I fingered
its new skin, the taut areola, so unlike
my twin breasts, three babies in,

so tired and easy in their wilt.
And another to the left of my right
nipple smaller than its sister,

like a girl-child biding its time,
darkening, rising slowly like bread
or warriors. I stood in the mirror

of a house I didn't know. I stood
in a body that had plans. All I knew
was to look for mouths to feed.

THE BLESSING

for my son

I have ignored you for a year.
I have not dwelt on the soft fur
of your arms or the way you rubbed
my cheek with your own starry cheek.

I splintered your hands away
from my heart when you exited
me. Of the men who have claimed
my body, only you reflect

my exact goodness, tragic
as a cotton field, ripe with bloom,
but I have not dwelt on this either.
Not in one year or three—

the way you break open your own
throat, singing, sculpting one world,
another, or kiss a girl in my kitchen,
calling her, *Love, My Love.* No:

I have ignored you for a year or six,
maybe. Not touching your feet
or your shoulders to dab them dry.
Not humming in your ear

as I did once. Not holding your head
against my chest in the sad night. I have not
dwelt on other women who speak sweetly
to you, laugh with you, or hold your head

against their chests in the sad night.
I have ignored you for a year or ten,
finally severing the root, purging,
drying out the heart: go.

THE PLIGHT OF LOVErs

You came to my body
in my wildest grief.
Drunk in it. I welcomed you.
There were catastrophes
I needed to explore.
You contained them all.

*

When you lap the well
of my blood, milky and flowing,
near the river and sugar cane fields,
you drink, too, my mother.
And her mother. And hers.
The lovers—each—they had.
This is the dowry.

*

This is the lot—
the only child I will give you
is myself. Be worthy:

I have eaten the rattlesnake.

acknowledgments & notes

From *A Tongue in the Mouth of the Dying* (University of Notre Dame Press 2013):
> "Preparing the Tongue," "Sundays after Breakfast: A Lesson in Cotton Picking," "Sundays after Breakfast: A Lesson in Speech," "Las Lenguas," "Summer," "Stray Cat," "Babies under the House," "My Mother Woke a Rooster," "Put Attention," "Ode to My Boots," "Morning Praise of Nightmares," "Wooden Box," "Mr. G's Collection," "Ode to El Cabrito," "Ancient Algebra," "Early Words for my Son," and "One Man's Name: Colonization of the Poetic, i-ix"

From *A Crown for Gumecindo* (Aztlan Libre Press 2015):
> "Where the Dead Come to Speak," "Love is Our Mother," "Praise Song for the Goat at the Grave," "The Absence of Water," "The Mesquite," "Without You, I am Cactus," "Newborns," "Día de los Muertos," "Sunday Dinner," "Stone Fruit," "Casketing," "Untouchable," untitled piece, "The Work," "En las Costillas de la Pagina," and "Goodbye Sonnet"

Many thanks to the editors of the following journals/anthologies who published earlier versions of the following poems:

Academy of American Poets/Poets.org: "The Blessing"
The Golden Shovel Anthology: New Poems Honoring Gwendolyn Brooks, edited by Peter Khan: "Play the Song"
Huizache: "Night Feeding"
Indiana Review: "Ode to the Beet"
The Map of Every Lilac Leaf, anthology edited by Matt Donovan: "So She Would Not Watch Him Split in Two, a Mother Commits her Child to the Care of Her Enemy"
Origins: "La Mano Ponderosa," "(To the) Young Girl on a Chair," "How to Sacrifice Your Son," and "The Miniature World of Faith"

Pariahs: Writing from Outside the Margins, edited by Sarah Rafael Garcia and <u>mónica teresa ortiz</u>: "Ars Politica"
POETRY: "Brownies of the Southwest" and "Last Meal"
What Saves Us: Poems of Empathy and Outrage in the Age of Trump, edited by Martín Espada: "Three Hundred Years Before These, Three Hundred Years After"

Also incredibly grateful for support from the Department of Arts & Culture at the city of San Antonio; the Language, Literature, and Art Department at Texas A&M University-San Antonio, Dr. Cynthia Teniente-Matson and Dr. Mirley Balasubramanya; Francisco Aragón and Letras Latinas at the University of Notre Dame; Martín Espada— for years in conversation and reflection; and my homies who held me up for seven years: Xelena Gonzalez, Sabrina San Miguel, Cecilia Macias, Scarlett Cerna, Bonnie Cisneros, Adrianna Santos, Alicia Reyes Barrientez, Julie and John Hodge, Amanda Keammerer, Rosalie Gomez, Dan Vera, Paul Lopez, Juan Luis Guzman, Jillian Flynn, Erin Oliver, Krystal Bosveld, Jen Barnard, and Diana Delgado. My mama & my daddy. And my babies, Drew, Vic, & Liv—all magic & fire—and their papa for unwavering support.

ABOUT THE AUTHOR

Laurie Ann Guerrero is the author of *A Tongue in the Mouth of the Dying* (Notre Dame 2013), *A Crown for Gumecindo* (Aztlan Libre Press 2015), and *Babies under the Skin*. Poet Laureate of San Antonio (2014 – 2016) and of Texas (2016 – 2017), Guerrero holds degrees from Smith College and Drew University and is the Writer-in-Residence at Texas A&M University-San Antonio.

Photo by Liv Garcés